Growing Up

by Nancy Day
illustrations by Bob Masugals

Scott Foresman
is an imprint of

PEARSON

Glenview, Illinois • Boston, Massachusetts • Chandler, Arizona
Upper Saddle River, New Jersey

Photographs

Every effort has been made to secure permission and provide appropriate credit for photographic material. The publisher deeply regrets any omission and pledges to correct errors called to its attention in subsequent editions.

Unless otherwise acknowledged, all photographs are the property of Pearson Education, Inc.

Photo locators denoted as follows: Top (T), Center (C), Bottom (B), Left (L), Right (R), Background (Bkgd)

12 Katrina Brown/Fotolia.

Illustrations Tracy Mattocks.

ISBN 13: 978-0-328-50826-6
ISBN 10:   0-328-50826-8

8 9 10 11 V010 17 16 15 14 13

five years old

eight years old

five weeks old

Dad came home with a box. "Look what I bought! Meet Pepper," he said.

Mom said, "What a great surprise!"

But Pepper ran over to Jun. The puppy jumped up. "No!" Jun cried.

"Don't be a baby," said Soo Mi.

"He is too big," said Jun.

Jun didn't like puppies jumping on him. He was still scared of dogs. Dad said, "It's okay. Soon you'll be bigger, and Pepper won't seem so scary."

"But so will Pepper!" said Jun. He wanted to be bigger than Pepper right now! Jun ran into the basement.

Jun didn't close the door. Pepper ran in after him. The puppy found Jun hiding behind the boxes. "No!" Jun shouted, "Don't jump."

Pepper just licked Jun's face. Jun was surprised. Pepper's tongue was pleasant. "This is probably a sign that you like me."

When Jun went off to school, Mom took Pepper to dog school. Jun learned his ABCs. Pepper learned not to jump up on people.

In school, Jun learned to count to 100.
Pepper learned how to go on walks.

Mom and Jun took Pepper for a walk.
Jun held on to the leash. He counted
all the way to 100 before Pepper pulled
him off the sidewalk.

Jun learned to give Pepper his food and keep his water dish filled. The big puppy followed Jun everywhere. Now, Jun didn't mind so much. He even bought treats for Pepper.

Jun and Soo Mi played catch in the backyard. Pepper caught the ball. "Give it back!" Soo Mi yelled as she chased the dog all over the yard.

Pepper ran to Jun. He dropped the ball at Jun's feet. "Good dog!" said Jun.

eight years old

five years old

six months old

One day Jun said, "Mom, Pepper keeps sneezing."

Pepper did not look happy. "Shall we take him to the vet?" Mom asked.

In her office, the vet pulled a bug out of Pepper's nose. Pepper wagged his tail.

"Remember how you used to be scared of Pepper?" Dad asked Jun.

Jun laughed. "He isn't a puppy anymore. He is a dog. I'm still a kid. But now I'm bigger. No matter how old we get, we will always be friends."

Pepper wagged his tail.

Dogs grow up faster than people. Puppies become adult dogs in one or two years, but human babies become adults in 21 years. Some people like to think that one "dog year" is the same as seven or more human years.

But small dogs live longer than big dogs. So a small dog's "dog year" is the same as about four human years. Other things can affect how long a dog lives. Some kinds of dogs live longer than others.

Some dog experts say a three-month-old puppy is like a five-year-old child. At six months, the puppy is like a ten-year old. At one year, the dog is like a teenager. At two, a dog is a full-grown "adult."

Think and Share

1. Reread page 10. What did Jun say Pepper keeps doing? Why did this happen? What did they do about it?

2. How did Jun feel about the puppy at the beginning of the story? How did Jun's feelings change by the end of the story?

3. Copy this chart on a separate sheet of paper. Write plural nouns from the story that end in -s, -es, and -ies. Write a sentence for each plural noun.

Ending	Noun	Sentence
-s		
-es		
-ies		

4. If you have a pet, tell how you help take care of it. If you don't have a pet, tell about a pet you would like to have.

Suggested levels for Guided Reading, DRA™,
Lexile,® and Reading Recovery™ are provided
in the Pearson Scott Foresman Leveling Guide.

Genre	Comprehension Skills and Strategy
Realistic fiction	• Cause and Effect • Character, Setting, and Plot • Story Structure

Scott Foresman Reading Street 2.2.4

Scott Foresman
is an imprint of

ISBN-13: 978-0-328-50826-6
ISBN-10:   0-328-50826-8

9 780328 508266

9 0 0 0 0 >

EMPOWERING CAMPUS MINISTRY

a condensed version of

Empowered

by the

Spirit

COMMITTEE ON EDUCATION
UNITED STATES CONFERENCE OF CATHOLIC BISHOPS